I Wish
You Good
Spaces

Other books by

Blue Mountain Arts inc.

Come Into the Mountains, Dear Friend
by Susan Polis Schutz
I Want to Laugh, I Want to Cry
by Susan Polis Schutz
Peace Flows from the Sky
by Susan Polis Schutz
Someone Else to Love
by Susan Polis Schutz
I'm Not That Kind of Girl
by Susan Polis Schutz
The Best Is Yet to Be
Step to the Music You Hear, Vol. I
Step to the Music You Hear, Vol. II
The Language of Friendship
The Language of Love
The Desiderata of Happiness
by Max Ehrmann
Whatever Is, Is Best
by Ella Wheeler Wilcox
Poor Richard's Quotations
by Benjamin Franklin
I Care About Your Happiness
by Kahlil Gibran/Mary Haskell
My Life and Love Are One
by Vincent Van Gogh
We Are All Children Searching for Love
by Leonard Nimoy
Catch Me with Your Smile
by Peter McWilliams

I Wish You Good Spaces

*Poetic selections
from the songs of*

Gordon
Lightfoot

*Edited by Susan Polis Schutz,
with Illustrations by Stephen Schutz*

Blue
Mountain
Arts T.M.
Boulder, Colorado

Library of Congress Number: 76-55842
ISBN: 0-88396-018-4

Lyrics reprinted with permission from
Warner Bros. Music, Los Angeles, Ca.
Layout and design by SandPiper Studios, Inc.

First Printing: July, 1977

 **Blue Mountain Arts** inc.
P.O. Box 4549   Boulder, Colorado 80306

Contents

"What a tale my thoughts could tell . . ."
Gordon Lightfoot

Introduction

The lyrics in contemporary music comprise some of the most beautiful poetry being written today—especially when the lyricist is someone like Gordon Lightfoot. A singer and composer, a minstrel and a poet, Gordon is a "one man band philosophical man" whose songs appeal to people of all ages and all walks of life.

Most of us became acquainted with Gordon Lightfoot and his music a little over ten years ago, shortly after he had written "Early Mornin' Rain." Since then he has become one of the world's most popular recording artists. At the present time, Gordon is composing a number of new songs, scratching and scribbling verses down on the backs of envelopes and napkins—lyrical jottings that will become tomorrow's gold records.

After listening to and loving Gordon's songs for so many years, reading his poetry now is like listening to a dear friend tell stories and talk of joy and love and life. I Wish You Good Spaces captures, on paper, the essence of his poetic expression. Susan Polis Schutz has selected a delightful arrangement of Lightfoot's lyrics, which are accompanied by the sensitive airbrush paintings of Stephen Schutz. As a harmonious blend of poetry, music and art, I Wish You Good Spaces is a unique and enjoyable collection.

Douglas Pagels

I wish you
good spaces
in the far away places
you go.
If it rains
or it snows,
may you be safe
and warm . . .
And if you need
somebody sometime,
you know I will
always be there.

*The lamp is burning low
upon my table top,
the snow is softly falling.
The air is still
in the silence of my room,
I hear your voice softly calling.
If I could only have you near . . .*

...Please cast away
the clothes you wear
and give your love to me . . .

Your smile
is like the golden sun,
I'd love to see you
laugh and run
as naked as the sea . . .

Go My Way
and I'll be
good to you.
Go My Way and your dreams
will all come true.
In the sunset,
the wild waves
are calling—
my shadow is following you . . .

Why must I sail my ship
alone without a friend?
My thoughts are on you
I dare not ask again . . .
Come on along
and together we'll go
Please, love me
and say that you'll be mine.

**T**he dead leaves
    of autumn
That cling so
    desperately
Must fly before the
cold October wind
Their simple life is ended
Must they be born to die again?

O, may the light
of freedom shine
For all the world
to see
And peace and joy
to all mankind
Through all the years
to be.

For soon the leaves will die
And the long hard wind will blow,
May this world
find a resting place
Where peaceful waters flow.

I f you go
into the forest,
gaze up through the leaves
and see the sky
that's almost wild.
You can learn to understand
what makes the forest
greet the man
like a mother's only child.

I just don't know
how you could be
anything but beautiful.
I think that I was
made for you,
and you were made for me.
And I know that
I will never change,
because we've been
friends through
rain or shine
for such a long, long time.

**T**hat's what you get
For lovin' me,
That's what you get
For lovin' me,
Well everything
you had is gone
As you can see,
That's what you get for lovin' me.

I ain't the kind
to hang around
With any new love
that I found
because moving
is my stock in trade
I'm moving on,
I won't think of you
when I'm gone.

So don't you shed
a tear for me,
I ain't the love
you thought I'd be,
I got a hundred
more like you,
So don't be blue,
I'll have a thousand
before I'm through.

Now, there you go
you're crying again,
Now, there you go
you're crying again,
But then, some day
when your poor heart
Is on the mend,
Well, I just might
pass this way again.

That's what you get
for lovin' me,
That's what you get
for lovin' me,
Well, everything you had
is gone
As you can see,
That's what you get
for lovin' me.

Rainy day people
always seem to know
when it's time to call;
rainy day people
don't talk,
they just listen
till they've heard it all.
Rainy day lovers don't
lie when they tell you
they been down like you;
rainy day people don't mind if
you're crying a tear or two.

If you get lonely all you really need
is that rainy day love;
rainy day people all know
there's no sorrow they can't
rise above.
Rainy day lovers don't
love any others,
that would not be kind;
rainy day people all know how
it hangs on your peace of mind.

Rainy day people always seem to know
when you're feeling blue;
high-stepping strutters who
land in the gutter
sometimes need one, too.
Take it or leave it or
try to believe it
if you been down too long;
rainy day lovers don't hide
love inside,
they just pass it on.

Laughing eyes and
smiling face;
it seems
so lucky just
to have the right
of telling you
with all my might
you're beautiful tonight.
And I know that
you will never stray,
because you've been that way
from day to day
for such a long,
long time.

Try to understand,
I'm not your
ordinary man,
still I can't deny
you go with me everywhere;
when I'm dreaming
you still share
my lonely nights . . .

And as I wander
to the cities and the towns,
I get so lonesome knowing
you could be around.
And when the show is over
there's a Holiday Motel,
and another empty bottle
and another tale to tell . . .

Try to comprehend,
I'm not your
ordinary friend.
At the end
of my life
I would pray
that I could be
returning to the shelter
of your love . . .

Try to understand,
I'm not your
ordinary man,
still I can't deny
you go with me
everywhere
like a shadow
in the gloom.
I remember all
the good times;
there's a ghost
in every room.

You make time stand still,
you do it now
and you always will.
You take me as I am,
you make me feel
like a brand new person . . .
because you are
what I am.

*I*n the
    early mornin' rain
With a dollar
    in my hand,
With an aching in my heart
And my pockets full of sand,
I'm a long way from home,
And I miss my loved ones so.
In the early mornin' rain,
With no place to go.

Out on runway number nine
Big seven-o-seven set to go,
But I'm stuck here in the grass
Where the cold wind blows.
Now the liquor tasted good,
And the women all were fast,
Well, there she goes, my friend,
She's rolling now at last.

Hear the mighty engines roar,
See the silver bird on high,
She's away and westward bound,
Far above the clouds she'll fly,
Where the mornin' rain don't fall,
And the sun always shines,
She'll be flying o'er my home
In about three hours time.

This old airport's got me down,
It's no earthly good to me,
Because I'm stuck here on the ground
As cold and drunk as I can be.
You can't jump a jet plane
Like you can a freight train,
So I'd best be on my way
In the early mornin' rain.

...L et us just
pretend awhile;
think about
the good things
now and then.

I think this time . . .
was the best time
that we two had ever known.
We tried the handle
of the house
upon the shore
and found the open door.
Once inside
we found a curious moonbeam
doing dances on the floor;
we were only playing
like two children
who had stayed
away from school . . .

Let us just pretend awhile;
think about the good things
now and then.

All you need is time,
all you need is time, time,
time to make me bend.

. . . All I need is trust,
all I need is trust, trust,
trust to make it show . . .

. . . All we need is faith,
all we need is faith,
faith to make it nice.

*There's peace in the garden,
there's peace in the air,
peace in the sound of the river.
There's peace in the meadow,
the sun shines like gold,
and if you were with me
there'd be peace
in my soul.*

 **I** see a place
　　where candles burn
and lovers
　　rest tonight.
The hollow sound
　　inside me now
keeps telling me to write.
But songs of love will never leave
love's feelings undefiled.
The tide has turned,
the waves roll in;
the waters fill my eyes.
The days fly by,
the waves roll in,
but freedom has not come.
I fear my faith will soon give out;
my senses come undone.
My role is played;
the demon dogs come stealing o'er the land.
And foolish, I would climb once more
a tree too weak to stand.

The price of lust has risen
until the ceiling will not stand.
The tears I shed were not in shame;
the world was in my hands.
If trust was just a simple thing,
then trusting I would be.
But deep within my soul
I know it's better to be free.
I see a place where candles burn
and lovers rest tonight.
The hollow sound inside me now
keeps telling me to write.
But songs of love should not be sung
where staying is not planned.
And foolish, I would climb once more
a tree too weak to stand.

remember when . . .
lovers would stick together,
when the days were warm
and the nights more tender,
when the bonds of truth
were not made to measure.

The fire
   is dying now,
my lamp
   is growing dim,
the shades
   of night
are lifting.
The morning light steals
across my window pane,
where webs of snow
are drifting.
If I could only
have you near . . .
I would be happy
just . . . to be once
again with you.

Behind the blue Rockies
the sun is declining
The stars they come stealing
at the close of the day.
Across the wide prairie
our loved ones lie sleeping
Beyond the dark forest
in a place far away . . .

There was a time in this fair land
when the railroad did not run,
When the wild majestic mountains
stood alone against the sun.
Long before the white man,
and long before the wheel
When the green dark forest
was too silent to be real.

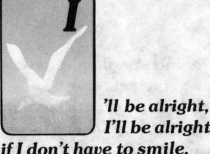

I'll be alright,
I'll be alright
if I don't have to smile,
If I don't have to face
the morning sunrise
for awhile.
I'll get along, you know,
I'll take tomorrow with a grin,
If I never have to think about
her love again . . .

Last night
she gave the final word,
she said
her last goodbye,
And disappeared forever
in the world outside.
One kiss
and then she took her leave to go
I know not where,
into the misty shadows
of the midnight air.
And I won't mind
if words are spoken
in empty love songs,
As long as
I don't have
to hear.
I'll be alright
if I don't have to
face the world again;
And if I never
love again,
I'll be alright.

If you could
read my mind,
love,
what a tale
my thoughts
could tell.
Just like an old time movie,
about a ghost from a wishing well.
In a castle dark or a fortress strong,
with chains upon my feet.
You know that ghost is me.
And I will never be set free as long as
I'm a ghost that you can't see.

If I could read your mind, love,
what a tale your thoughts could tell.
Just like a paperback novel,
the kind the drugstores sell.
Then you reached the part
where the heartaches come,
the hero would be me.
But heroes often fail,
and you won't read that book again
because the ending's just
too hard to take!
I'd walk away like a movie star
who gets burned in a three-way script.

Enter number two:
A movie queen to play the scene
of bringing all the good things
out of me.
But for now, love, let's be real;
I never thought I could feel this way
and I've got to say that I just don't get it.
I don't know where we went wrong,
but the feeling's gone
and I just can't get it back.

If you could read my mind, love,
what a tale my thoughts could tell.
Just like an old time movie,
about a ghost from a wishing well.
In a castle dark or a fortress strong,
with chains upon my feet.

But stories always end,
and if you read between the lines,
you'd know that I'm just trying to
understand the feelings that you lack.
I never thought I could feel this way
and I've got to say
that I just don't get it.
I don't know where we went wrong,
but the feeling's gone
and I just can't get it back.

... *I* got to thinking
what makes you want to go
to know the wherefore and the why . . .

Come on, sunshine,
what can you show me?
Where can you take me
to make me understand?

The wind can shake me,
brothers forsake me.
The rain can touch me,
but can I touch the rain?

Then all at once it came to me;
I saw the wherefore,
and you can see it if you try.

It's in the sun above,
It's in the one you love;
you'll never know the reason why.

Will you
　　gather daydreams,
or will you
　　gather wealth?
How can you find your fortune
if you cannot find yourself?

f people
could look into
each other's eyes
What a wonderful place
this world would be.
All strife would end,
we could start again . . .

*Let's steal away
in the noonday sun;
it's time for a
summertime dream.
On a trip on down
to wonderland
in love among the flowers
where time gets lost . . .
it's time for a
summertime dream.*

It's so nice
to meet
an old friend
and pass the time of day,
and talk about the hometown
a million miles away.
Is the ice still in the river?
Are the old folks still the same?
And by the way,
did she mention my name?

Did she mention my name
just in passing?
And looking at the rain
do you remember
if she dropped a name or two?
Is the home team still on fire?
Do they still win all the games?
And by the way,
did she mention my name?

Is the landlord still a loser?
Do his signs hang in the hall?
Are the young girls still as pretty
in the city in the fall?
Does the laughter on their faces
still put the sun to shame?
And by the way,
did she mention my name?

Did she mention my name
just in passing?
And when the talk ran high
did the look in her eye
seem far away?
Is the old roof still leaking
when the late snow turns to rain?
And by the way,
did she mention my name?

Did she mention my name just in passing?
And looking at the rain
do you remember
if she dropped a name or two?
Won't you say hello from someone?
There'll be no need to explain.
And by the way,
did she mention my name?

**G**o first
      in the world,
go forth
      with your fears,
remember a price must be paid.
Be always too soon,
be never too fast
at the time when all
bets must be laid.
Beware of the darkness,
be kind to your children,
remember the woman who waits . . .

When you're caught by the gale
and you're full under sail,
beware of the dangers below.
And the song that you sing
should not be too sad,
and be sure not to sing it too slow.

*F*orgive me
the ways of my heart;
Don't try to pretend
or lend me your love.
Don't ask of me
what you wouldn't
ask yourself . . .
Don't make me do what you wouldn't
do yourself.

Forgive me
the bad things I do;
Don't ask me to change or
exchange what I am
for something else,
you know that wouldn't do.
If time gets too heavy
and you can no longer bear it,
and you need someone to share it,
Well, tell me . . .
I'll try to make amends.

Forgive me
my unsettled ways;
Don't linger in time
or finger what's mine.
Don't make me do what you wouldn't
do yourself . . .

I'm not ashamed
to say
that I've
loved you well . . .

*Friends are for sorting
out the hangups that we hide;*

*Walls are for shutting out
the love we feel inside . . .*

 **I'm not ashamed
to listen to
the fast falling rain
in the morning
upon my window.
I'm not afraid to cry,
I'm not ashamed to try
to be your friend once again,
that's what friends are for.
Friends are for explaining the mistakes
we might have made . . .**

I'm not saying that I love you
I'm not saying that I'll care.
If you love me
I'm not saying that I'll care.
I'm not saying I'll be there
When you want me.
Now I may not be alone
Each time you see me,
Along the street or in a small cafe,
But still I won't deny you
Or mistreat you
Baby, if you'll let me have my way.
I'm not saying I'll be sorry
For all the things that I might say
That make you cry.
I can't say I'll always do
The things you want me to.
I'm not saying I'll be true
But I'll try.

I *understand you perfectly,*
there is no way that I can see
you living by yourself . . .
I must be with you constantly
Your presence means so much to me,
much more than
life itself.

 **You got places
to go,
you got people
to see;
still I'm gonna miss you.**

But anyway,

I wish you
   good spaces
      in the
far away
places
      you go . . .

   And if
      you need
somebody
sometime,
   you know
         I will
   always
   be there.

About the Author

As one of the most popular and respected names in contemporary music, Gordon Lightfoot is a sensitive songwriter and lyricist, a concert performer and a world-renowned recording artist. His music, with its roots intertwined in early folk music, has blossomed into a style unique to Gordon Lightfoot. His melodies—from "Early Mornin' Rain" to "The Wreck of the Edmund Fitzgerald"—have received many laurels over the years; his songs have been performed and recorded by hundreds of musical artists, and he has been the recipient of various musical awards including Grammy nominations and gold records.

Gordon's story is that of the "overnight success backed with years of hard work." His first vocal performance took place in his hometown of Orillia, Ontario, at the age of seven, and he has been entertaining ever since. After high school, he attended Westlake College of Music where he studied orchestration for a time, before returning to the Toronto region, which has become his home. When he first began his musical career, he explains that, "I knew six guitar chords and some variations. I had some piano theory, which helped with the writing, but usually I just played by ear."

Eventually, Gordon mastered both the six and twelve-string guitars, and he began playing professionally in bars and coffee houses. "Playing in bars had its advantages," he recalls. "You could try out all kinds of new things and make all kinds of mistakes and hardly anyone noticed . . . it was paid rehearsal." And it paid off. One night, folksingers Ian and Sylvia caught his act — were extremely impressed with Gordon's musical creations — and they introduced him to friends in the management and recording industry. Gordon signed with United Artists in 1965 and recorded five albums over a four-year period. He later signed with Warner/Reprise, and he has recorded on their label since 1969. To date, Gordon has recorded more than sixteen albums, and he has written nearly five hundred songs over the past thirteen years.